A VISION OF
HELL

Tortured Souls in Hell

CAROL J. CARVER

BALBOA.PRESS

A DIVISION OF HAY HOUSE

Balboa Press books may be ordered through booksellers or by contacting:

Balboa Press
A Division of Hay House
1663 Liberty Drive
Bloomington, IN 47403
www.balboapress.com
844-682-1282

Scripture taken from KJV

Print information available on the last page.

ISBN: 979-8-7652-3117-3 (sc)
ISBN: 979-8-7652-3118-0 (e)

Balboa Press rev. date: 07/18/2022

As with each and every book that I write, I want to dedicate this to God, my Heavenly Father, and Jesus Christ, His Son, that loves and saved me from the hell I wrote about.

And many thanks…
To Balboa Publishing Company for publishing my books. You gave of your time to help me. I am grateful. Self-publishing is not easy for me. I wouldn't have made it this far if it hadn't been for Ron B. Your guidance, typing, and encouragement is deeply appreciated. God richly bless you. I have a faithful person who did the editing for me. She was a blessing to take the time from her busy schedule to help me. I wish God's best for you.

Author's Note: on "Alleluia", from Heavenly Visions,

On page 33 I want to explain. When I was in Heaven, I always heard "Alleluia", with an A, not an H. This is true, but let me tell you Halleluiah is still said with an H. Somehow this was left out of my book. I deeply apologize.

INTRODUCTION

I was allowed to see heaven so I could write about my experience of seeing it. It is a beautiful place to be, to see, and to hope to go there. I talk to a lot of people that want to go there, they just don't want to go there yet.

Talking to people about becoming a Christian isn't always easy and can be a life-changing process.

As I read the King James Bible I found more Scriptures about hell than I did about heaven. It is a person's choice where you want to spend eternity. God doesn't force you to go to either place. "For God so loved the world, that He gave His only Son...." John 3:16 (KJV)

It's up to each individual what we will do with Jesus Christ in our lives. Life isn't always easy. People ask me if heaven is real - what about hell?

As I already mentioned in my Heavenly Visions book, I am extremely curious about things. When I read the Bible, I wonder how the people were dressed, what the location looked like, what foods did they eat, how did they get along, and did they regret the decisions they made?

My dad was an evangelist, worked a full-time job, and raised and trained show horses. He told me to "think before I speak", but the trouble is, more often than not, I speak before I think.

People ask me about hell. My only knowledge of it was what I read in the King James Bible. So, I asked God if he'd let me see it.

He told me to fast and pray and He'd allow me to see it so I could write a book about it.

I did see it. It must have made the devil furious because I had a stroke and was in the hospital for three days after I saw it. During those three days I asked God if I could go to heaven, but he told me, "No, I have work for you to do." It is extremely important to know Bible Scriptures because I used them to fight the devil for my mind due to the stroke.

At home, my husband, Floyd, who was always so strong, became physically and spiritually weak. I didn't understand what was happening at first. As time went on, I was told by a doctor he had dementia, then Alzheimer's. Later, he died in January 2020. Alzheimer's is a terrible disease, and the person can be cruel to their caregiver. My prayers go to you all that take care of your loved ones with it. Getting through all of this held me back from being able to write the book of what I saw about hell.

A lot of times I heard people say we have hell on earth. We go through trials that aren't easy, but it isn't the hell the Bible talks about. Believe me. I've seen it. It is horrible. Let me tell you what I've seen.

MY VISION OF HELL

CHAPTER 1

People have different ideas about hell. Especially people that don't read The Bible. Some people think there isn't an eternal hell because it is a hell on earth, and life isn't fair. Some people told me they think hell is a party place because they will be with their friends.

One guy told me to come to his funeral. I should put a cigarette in one of his hands and a beer bottle in the other hand, have a jukebox there, and let the people dance to loud music to have fun.

My prayer is for people to know the truth. I read the scriptures in The Bible. Some people don't believe The Bible or me. The Scriptures tell us what hell is like. It has no rest, only pain, sorrows, and torment. No communication, burning heat, and they do not feel the presence of God.

Who will go there? The scripture states in Revelation 3:5 (KJV), "Whosoever will not accept Jesus Christ, and their name is not written in the Book of Life" will be in hell.

I asked God to show me hell. He told me to fast with no food, only water for three days. I did as he told me.

At the end of three days, he sent an angel to me. He looked seven feet tall, appeared masculine, strong, had wings… He was handsome, and his whole entity was a brilliant white. He did not tell me his name, though I did ask him. He held on to me as we traveled at a rapid speed to the center of the earth (as I was told by the angel). We went into the water which was so dark I could not see except for the brightness of the angel. We came to a black metal gate that was locked. There are four gates: East, West, North, and South entrances.

This is what it looked like to me:

A spirit, a fallen angel, was a guard at the gate. He was told by the angel of God that we were sent there by God, and to let us inside. The guard was dressed all in black. The guard opened the gate all the while using filthy language because he hates God, His angels, and His people. I heard him speaking but the angel of God told me that God protected me from understanding what he said. I could feel the hate he had for us.

The angel of God and I entered a hallway that had a red carpet like the celebrities use here. As we walked down the hallway, we could see on each side were locked doors. I could hear horrible screams. I put my hands over my ears which didn't help at all. In the spirit realm a spirit can hear. The smell was so bad it was horrific. A burning sulphureous pit. A lack of air made it hard for me to breathe. I was told by the angel of God I could only breathe and survive because of God.

We walked to a room where I saw a beautiful angel that didn't have wings looking at us. He sat on a white chair with the arms of the chair curved. The shape of a lion was on each arm. Red rubies were the eyes of the lion. Satan was smiling at us. He had on a big red ruby ring.

I knew we were in hell, and he was the devil. Satan stood up still smiling, pointed his finger at me and said, "Welcome to my kingdom, to my heaven." [He does not call it hell.] "Go see my kingdom then, come back to tell me what you think about it."

From reading the Bible I know he desires to be God Almighty.

> How are thou fallen from heaven, o Lucifer, son of the morning: How art thou cut down to the ground, which did weaken the nations: For thou hast said in thine heart, I will ascend into heaven, I will exalt my throne above the stars of God: I will sit also upon the mount of the congregation, in the sides of the north: I will ascend above the heights of the clouds; I will be like The Most High. Yet thou shall be brought down to hell, to the sides of the pit. They that see thee shall narrowly look upon thee, and consider thee, saying, Is this the man that made the earth to tremble, that did shake kingdoms; That made the world as a wilderness, and destroyed the cities thereof; that opened not the house of his prisoners?

Isaiah 14:12-17 (KJV)

CHAPTER 2

The angel of God never left me or took his arm from around me. I felt fear and wanted to escape from there. I was told by God's voice that I was shown hell so I could write a book to warn people to avoid hell at all costs.

People will feel the degree of heat from the fire in accordance with the weight of their sins.

The angel of God took me back to the hallway with the red carpet. As I said before it was dark, and I could only see by the angel's brightness. All of the doors were locked. The angel took me through a door into a room that smelled like death, and the screams were horrible to hear. They were tormented souls with no way out. It was a pit where they were always moving - with no rest.

By the light of the angel, I saw what I knew was a male who was moving constantly. I was allowed to ask him why he was there. "I'm here because I did not give up lust for women while I was on earth. It led me to people I enjoyed being with. Oh, God gave me opportunities to accept Jesus Christ, but I chose the lust. I died and came here. I'm angry at God for taking away my pleasures. Here in this pit, you think of the thought of your sin, but you can't accomplish it; then, you feel the fire, pain, and scream in agony. It is awful. And it is torment to have memories of our sins, knowing why we are here; Satan doesn't let us forget them. Satan and his demons laugh at us, torment us, and remind us how foolish we were. They are hideous demons. Go back and tell the people not to have lust. Everyone here knows that God in The Bible spoke the truth. One day we will leave here to be in the lake of fire for all eternity. We dread it but we can't change it. We resent God for it. The Bible states:

> "the fearful, and the unbelieving, and the abominable, and murderers, and whoremongers, and sorcerers, and idolaters, and all liars, shall have their part in the lake which burns with fire and brimstone: which is the second death."

> Revelation 21:8 (KJV),

CHAPTER 3

I have the knowledge to know that God knows who every person is and where they are, but they cannot feel the presence of God or Jesus Christ. The rejection they gave to Them they now feel themselves.

God means what He says and says what He means. It is too late to help these lost souls. There is no escaping out of hell. There is no purpose. No one to comfort them. No conversation between them. They can hear each other's screams in the same room. It is torment for them to have the knowledge that there is a heaven, and their loved ones are there, but they are not there with them.

Smelling the sulphureous orders and feeling what heat from the fire that I did, must be horrible for them. I can't comprehend it.

CHAPTER 4

God allowed me to enter another room and ask a female {spirit} why she was here. "I was a good person. I knew about God and Jesus Christ. The cares of the world got me too busy for them. I became luke-warm and went on not caring. I died and came here ashamed; and angry at God for making hell and the devil. I remember all the opportunities I could have had to witness for Christ, but I didn't. I can't go back to change it, and I don't have a future to look forward to."

> "Because thou art luke-warm, and neither cold nor hot, I will spue thee out of my mouth." Spue in the Youngs Concordance means to vomit.
>
> Revelation 3:16 (KJV)

I'm so glad that the Lord told me not to eat any food before I saw hell because I'd have been sick if God had not had the wisdom to tell me to fast first.

God doesn't send a person to hell without having an opportunity to hear about and accept Jesus Christ. God is just and loving. He cares about people. There are no second opportunities. It isn't about chances but rather is about accepting Jesus Christ.

CHAPTER 5

The next room we entered was also dark with screams, the sulphureous order, and no rest for them as had been in all the other rooms. In this room I was shown all kinds of gambling devices. I believe I was allowed to see them in my mind. I was allowed to ask a male spirit why he was here. This is what he told me: "I was a gambler while I lived on earth. I didn't want to take the time for Jesus Christ. I wanted money but I really didn't care if I won or lost. Gambling was my addiction.

When I died my name wasn't found in the Book of Life, so I was escorted here by one of Satan's angels. It is horrible here. I blame God for it all. Why did he make the devil in the first place? All of us here desire to gamble. We see what we like to gamble with in our minds, but we can't touch them. Then, we feel the fire and scream. What torment for God to put on us. We were only human. None of us are perfect."

Excuses won't do. God gave us His word, The Bible, Jesus Christ, and the Holy Spirit. I feel sad that I cannot help anyone in hell.

CHAPTER 6

As we entered the next room it seemed to me that the screams were louder. I felt tremendous hate as I heard screams of voices saying: "I hate you!"

In a second of time, I saw guns, knives, and all kinds of weapons to kill people with. These people desired to kill but couldn't achieve it. They also had the memories of whom they had already killed. I was told by the angel of God that anger, cussing, strife, bitterness, and unforgiveness are locked in this room.

No one repents in hell. It is utter darkness and despair. They want to be out of there but know they must stay. There is no love, no water anywhere, and no friends or family to comfort them, only their pain.

Hell is a place where Satan controls all. The smell of death is everywhere. Demons are scary and dangerous. They can't get away from them. They fear what they can do to them. The next room is where you feel their loneliness. No peace is in any place. Loneliness is felt so strong you can feel terror. It is a horrible feeling.

I viewed other rooms of alcohol, sex, drugs, lying, stealing, rapists, and whatever sins are in the world. Spirits or demons tormented these lost souls. We cannot imagine their pain. It is so great. All of it is overwhelming.

Hearing all the screams and smelling the smells was getting unbearable to me. Not a prayer can help them now. The greater their sins - the greater they feel the fire. I asked the angel if we could leave. He told me I had to face Satan to tell him what he wanted to hear.

Again, we walked on the red carpet down the hallway to the room where Satan was sitting. He looked like a beautiful angel smiling at me. I didn't see any wings on him. I looked into his eyes as he said,

"What do you think of my kingdom? My heaven?" He stretched out his arms as if to represent it all.

Up to this time I hadn't spoken a word to Satan, and I didn't want to now. I asked the angel of God if we could leave. He told me we could not leave until I told Satan my answer. I wanted to get it over with, so I looked back into Satan's eyes realizing he was waiting for my answer. He smiled, looking at me. He said: "Name anything you want. I'll give it to you. What do you want? Money? Prestige? What would you like to have? All you need to do is to tell me that you'll denounce Jesus Christ."

I was still looking into his eyes. "I don't want anything you have to offer me. I still choose Jesus Christ."

Satan stood up, pointed his finger at me, screamed with his face turning red and he shrieked loudly, "I hate you! I hate God! I will make it hard for you. Wait and see." He was cursing God.

> And there was war in heaven. Michael and his angels fought against the dragon, and the dragon fought and his angels, And prevailed not, neither was their place found anymore in heaven. And the great dragon was cast out, that old serpent, called the devil, and satan, which deceiveth the whole world; he was cast out into the earth and his angels were cast out with him. And I heard a loud voice saying in heaven, "now is come salvation, and strength, in the kingdom of our God, and the power of his Christ; for the accuser of our brethren is cast down, which accused them before our God day and night.
>
> Revelation 12: 7-10 (KJV)

If you think Satan can help you, just remember he can't help himself. And if you think the ones in hell have remorse and want to repent, you are badly mistaken. They don't want to be in hell, but they are angry at God for making hell. Not one soul told me they wanted to repent or wished they had lived differently to be in heaven. Resentment for God and Jesus Christ were felt in every room.

I saw and heard enough so I asked the angel of God if we could leave now. As he was still holding on to me, we went back out the hallway, out to the gate we came in, and saw 'the guard'. The angel of God told him to unlock the gate, which he did, again, using foul language.

We were in the water. It was dark all around us. I could see by the brightness of the angel the water was cold, but it didn't bother me.

We traveled through the atmosphere at a rapid speed. We were at my house. The angel disappeared in front of my eyes. People have asked me what state of mind I was in when I went to see hell. I believe it was my spirit. I say that because I don't believe my flesh could have withstood the horrible heat.

The devil will promise you things, but he is a liar. In the book of John we read:

> "Ye are of your father the devil, and the lusts of your father ye will do. He was a murderer from the beginning, and abode not in the truth, because there is no truth in him. When he speaketh a lie, he speaketh of his own: for he is a liar, and the father of it."

John 8:44 (KJV)

What a contrast compared to what Heaven is like with almighty God and Jesus Christ.

> The children [sinners] of the kingdom [of satan] shall be cast out into outer darkness: there shall be weeping and gnashing of teeth.

Matthew 8:12 (KJV)

After I had seen hell and was home, I felt sad for everyone there knowing they can't be helped. I felt sick remembering the demons' smells, locked rooms, and the fire. Weeping and gnashing of teeth isn't a party. Total darkness is not seeing anyone except demons.

CHAPTER 7

HELL

All of the scriptures are in the King James version of the Holy Bible. They are not new scriptures. Don't be deceived. God means exactly what he says.

One day, face to face, you will see Jesus Christ. In Revelation it states,

> "and I saw the dead, small and great, standing before God; and the books were opened! And another book was opened, which is the Book of Life; and the dead were judged all of those things which were

written in the books, according to their works."

Revelation 20:12(KJV)

The most frightening statement an individual could ever hear would be Christ looking into their eyes on Judgment Day saying: "I never knew you; depart from me."

That is an eternal separation from God.

Matthew 7:23 (KJV)

Hell is marked before him, and destruction has no covering.

Job 26:6 (KJV)

The wicked shall be turned into hell, and all the nations that forget God.

Psalm 9:17 (KJV)

Let deaths siege upon them, and let them go down quick into hell; for wickedness is in their dwellings, and among them.

Psalm 55:15 (KJV)

For a fire is kindled in my anger, and shall burn unto the lowest hell, and shall consume

the earth with her increase, and set on fire
the foundations of the mountains.

Deuteronomy 32:22 (KJV)

The sorrows of hell, compassed me about,
the snares of death prevented me.

II Samuel 22:6 (KJV)

The sorrows of death compassed me, and
the pains of hell got hold upon me; I found
trouble and sorrow.

Psalm 116:3 (KJV)

Therefore, hell hath enlarged herself, and
opened her mouth without measure: in their
Glory, and their multitude, and their pomp,
and he that rejoiceth, shall descend unto it.

Isaiah 5:14 (KJV)

Hell and destruction are before The Lord:
how much more than the hearts of the
children of men.

Proverbs 15:11 (KJV)

Hell and destruction are never full; so the
eyes of man who are never satisfied.

Proverbs 27:20 (KJV)

And I say also unto thee, that thou art Peter, and unto this Rock I will build my church, and the gates of hell shall not prevail against it.

Matthew 16:18

I am he that liveth, and was dead; and behold, I am alive forever more, Amen; and have the keys of hell and death.

Revelation 1:18 (KJV)

And death in hell were cast into the Lake of Fire. This is the second death.

Revelation 20:14 (KJV)

And whoever was not found written in the Book of Life was cast into Lake of Fire.

Revelation 20:15 (KJV)

Hell is total darkness: no love, no presence of God, and no communication with anyone. The devil is at war with God, thinking he will win, deceiving himself. God created the devil. The devil cannot help himself. At God's appointed time:

And the devil that deceived them was cast into the Lake of Fire and brimstone, where the beast and the false prophet are, and

shall be tormented day and night forever
and ever.

Revelation 20:10 (KJV)

God didn't promise us our lives would be easy, but he
promised to be with us, to have eternal life, and heaven to
go to. What will your life be when you face Christ?

CHAPTER 8

HOPE

If you would like to accept Jesus Christ, here are scriptures to help you. You aren't the only one that has sinned:

> As it is written, there is not one righteous, no, not one
>
> Romans 3:10 (KJV)
>
> For all hath sinned, and come short of the Glory of God,
>
> Romans 3:23 (KJV)

Wherefore, as by one man sin entered into the world, and death by sin; and so death passed upon all men, for that all sinned;

Romans 5:12 (KJV)

For the wages of sin is death; and the gift of god is eternal life through Jesus Christ our Lord.

Romans 6:23 (KJV)

Hope in Jesus Christ

But God commandeth his love towards us, in that, while we were yet sinners, Christ died for us.

Romans 5:8 (KJV)

That if thou shall confess with thy mouth thy Lord Jesus, and shall believe in thy heart that God has raised him from the dead, you shall be saved. For with the heart man believeth unto righteousness; and with the mouth confession is made unto salvation. For the scripture saith, whosoever believeth on him shall not be ashamed. And there is no difference between the Jew and the Greek: for the same Lord over all is rich unto all that call upon him. For whosoever

shall call upon the name of the Lord shall
be saved.

Romans 10:9-13 (KJV)

For God so loved the world, that he gave
his only begotten Son, that whosoever
believeth on Him should not perish, but
have everlasting life.

John 3:16 (KJV)

I know I have written what I've seen, to tell you hell is
real. And I've written a lot of scriptures. The visions I've seen
won't save your souls, only Christ can tell you the truth.
That's why I've written them.

His (Christ) going forth is from the end of
the heaven, and His circuit to the end of
it: and there's nothing hid from the heat
thereof. The law of the Lord is perfect,
converting the soul; the testimony of the
Lord is sure, making wise the simple. The
statutes of the Lord are right, rejoicing the
heart: the commandment of the Lord is pure,
enlightening the eyes. The fear of the lord
is clean, enduring forever: the judgments of
the Lord are true and righteous altogether.
1 More to be desired are they than gold,
yes, than much fine gold: sweeter also than
honey and the honeycomb. Moreover by

them is thy servant warned: and in keeping
of them there is great reward.

Psalm 19:6-11 (KJV)

If you read this and know you need to be forgiven of
your sins, ask Jesus Christ to forgive you.

For God so loved the world, that he gave
his only begotten son, that whosoever
believes in Him should not perish, but have
everlasting life.

John 3:16 (KJV)

You have the opportunity to accept Jesus Christ and
be on your way to heaven. Hell is real. Ask God all of your
questions. He longs to fellowship with you. Little short
sentences to a long conversation.

Find a church to go to. Pray they teach the truth. Pray.
Read The Bible. Trust God one day at a time. One second
at a time. One thought at a time.

Receive His peace that goes beyond human
understanding. Know how much Jesus Christ loves you.
Nothing has been said or done that He hasn't seen or heard
before. You can fully trust Him.

In Closing

When I read John 3:16, I thought about the whole world and that made Jesus Christ seem so far away for me. As I continued to read the Scriptures, Jesus Christ did speak to the multitudes but many times He ministered to just one person. That brought Jesus Christ to me personally which is an awesome thought. I know He loves me, but He has time for you also. He loves you too. In Malachi it states:

> And they that feared The Lord spoke one to another: and The Lord harkened, and heard it, in the book of remembrance was written before Him for them that fear The Lord, and that thought upon His name. And they shall be mine, saith The Lord of Hosts, in that day when I make up my jewels; and I will spare them, as a man spears his own

son that serves him. Then shall ye return, and discern between the righteous and the wicked, between him that serves God and him that serves Him not.

Malachi 3:16-18

I have also visited Heaven, after which I wrote a book called "Heavenly Visions".

Printed in the United States
by Baker & Taylor Publisher Services